SUMMER
WRITE &
DRAW
JOURNAL FOR
KIDS

THIS BOOK BELONGS TO:

....

FOR THE SUMMER OF:

....

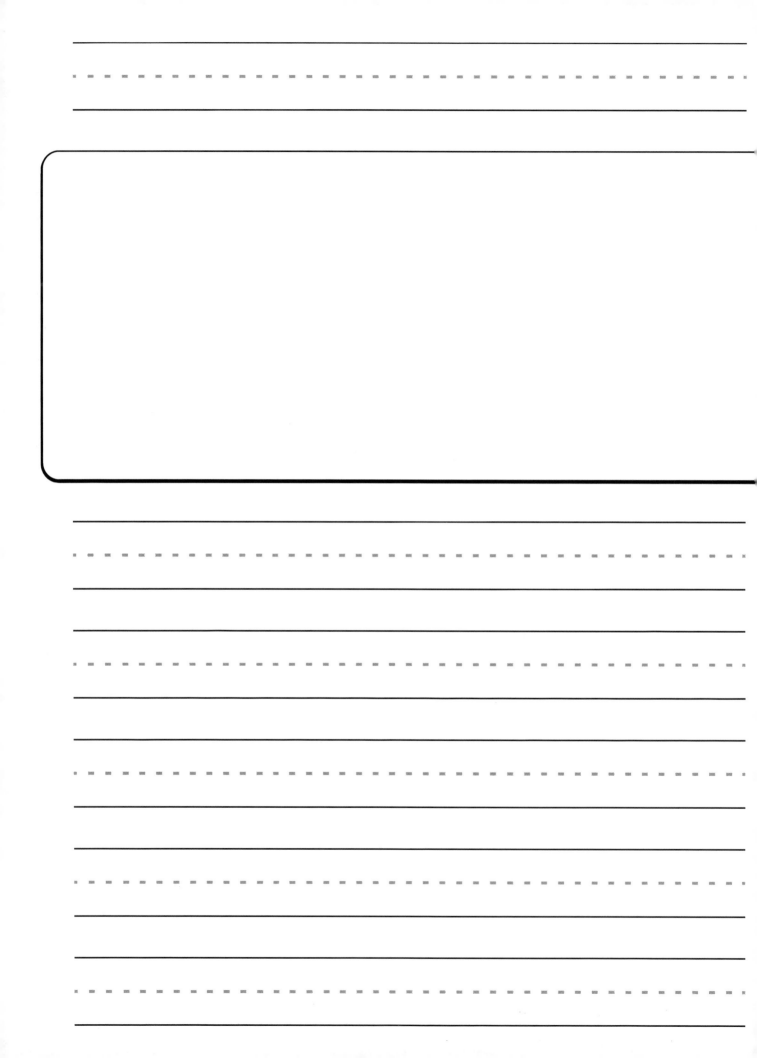

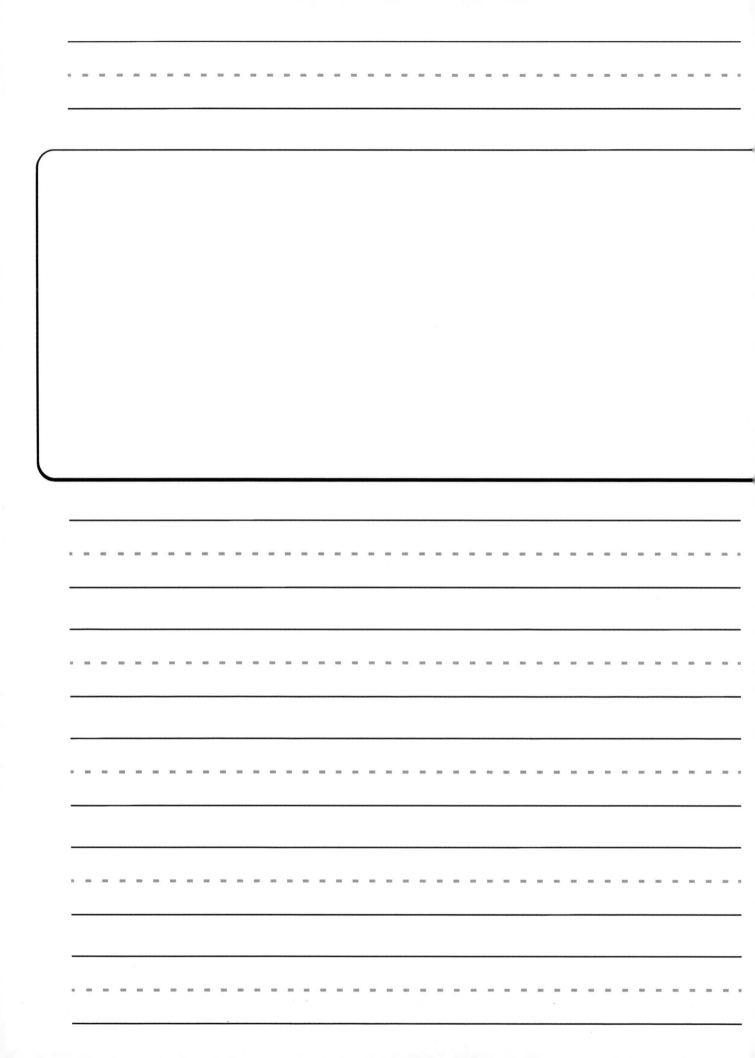

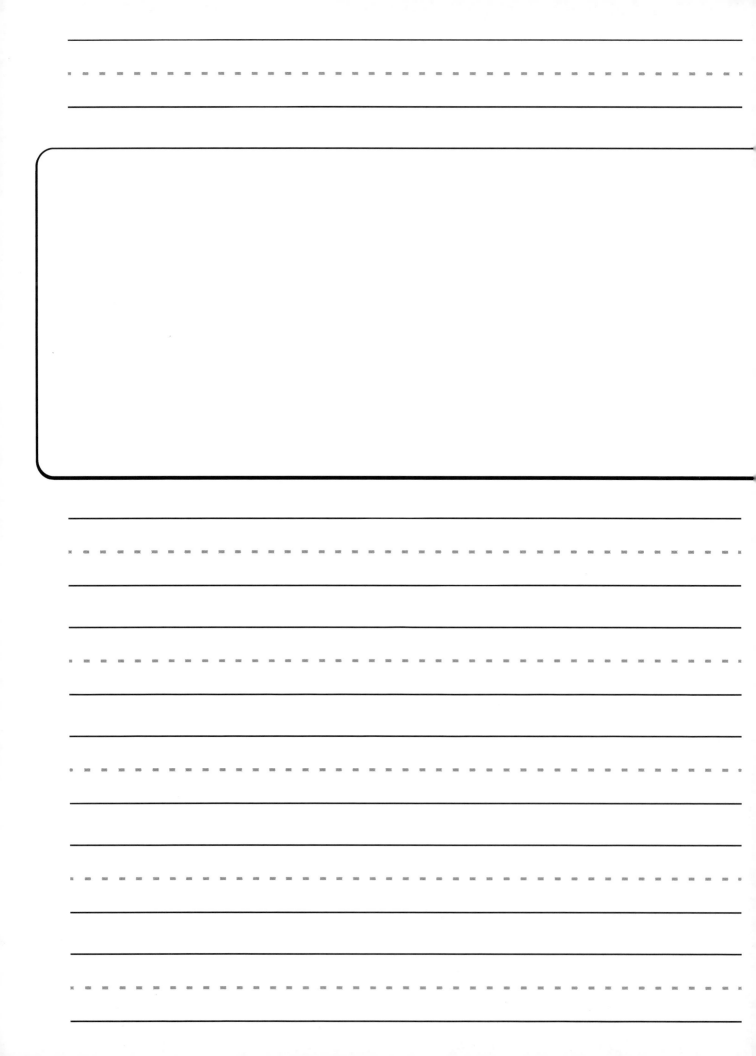

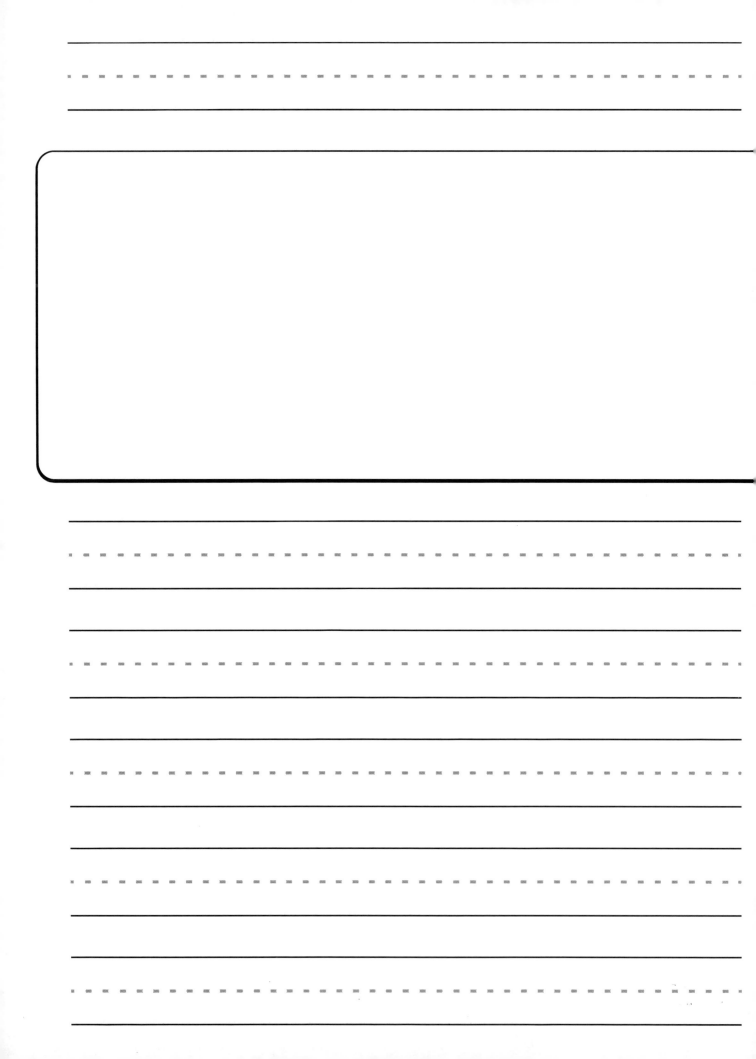

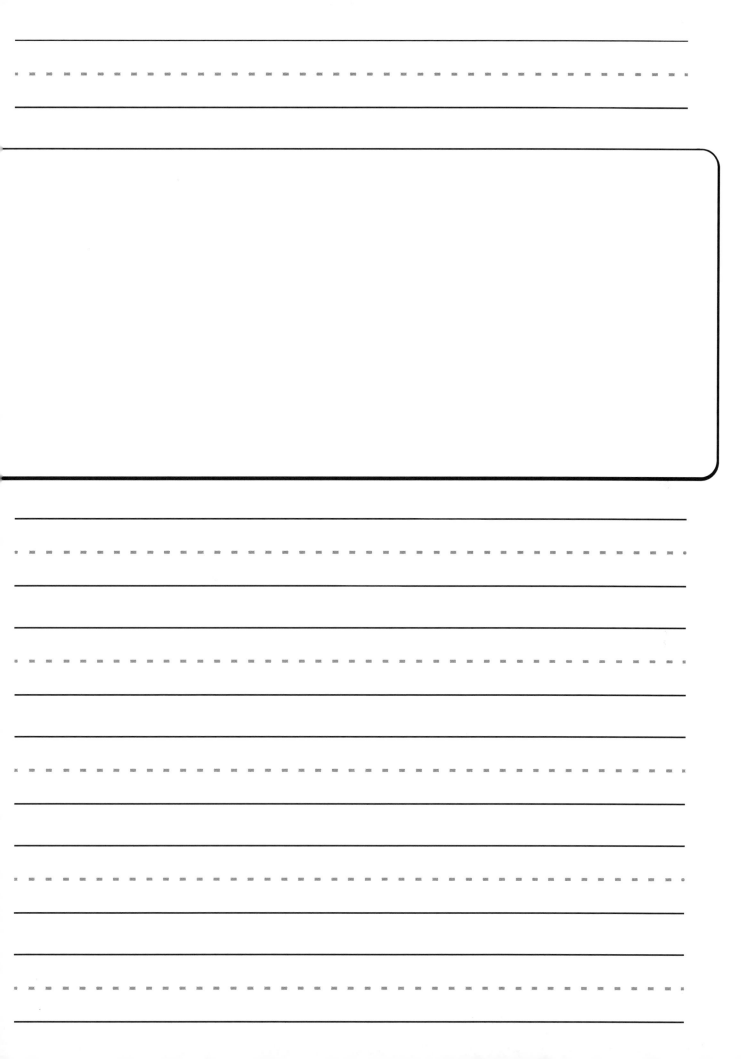

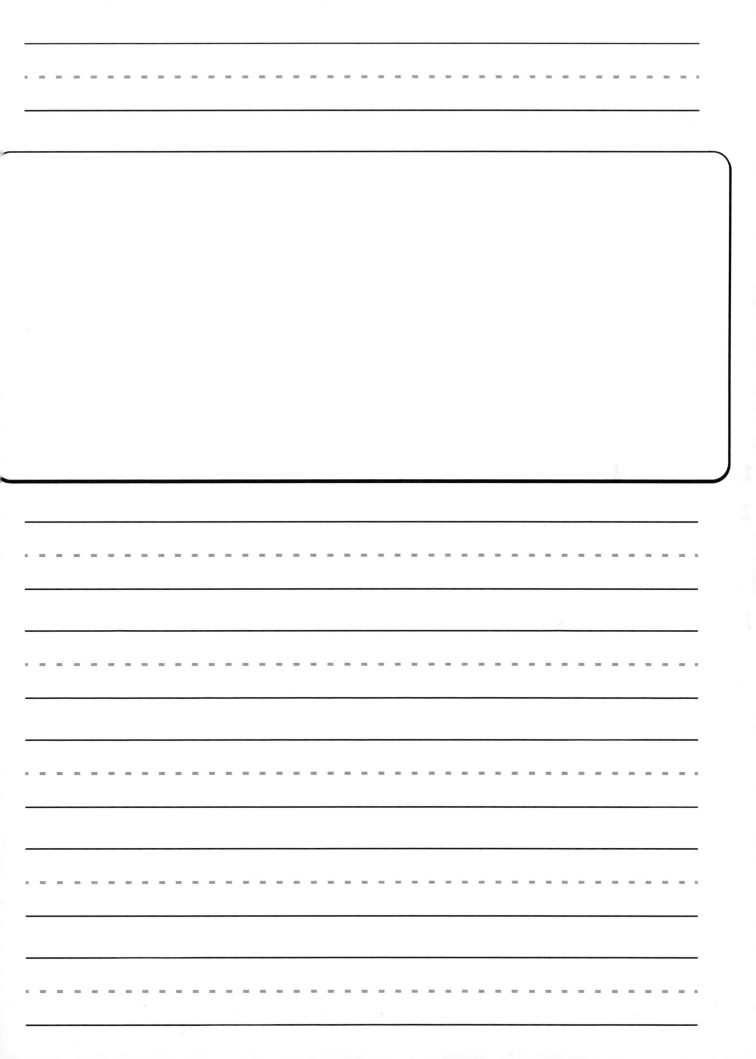

Other Notebooks and Educational Coloring Book from CuteNotebooksandJournals.com:

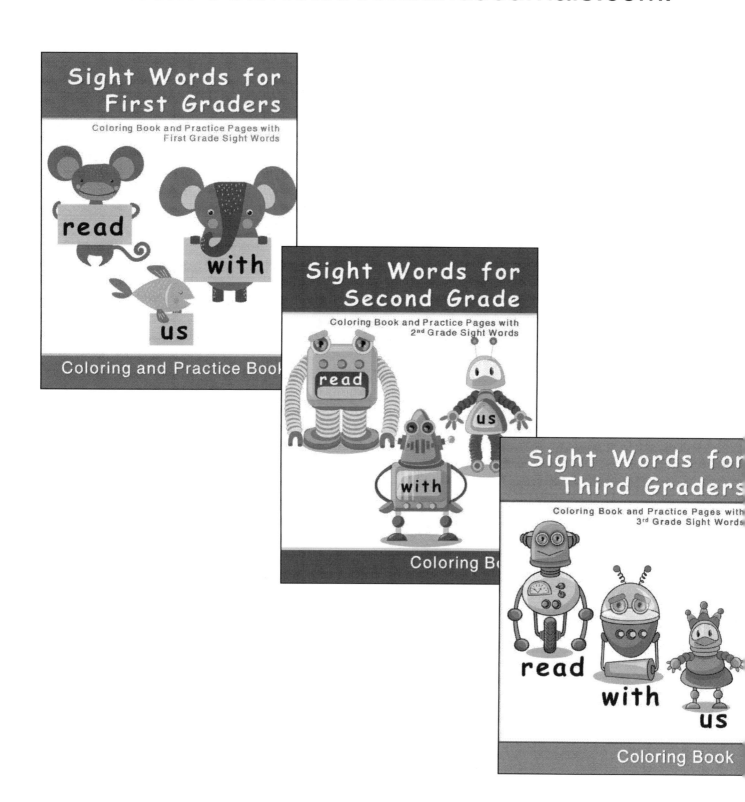

Made in the USA
Las Vegas, NV
28 May 2021

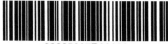